D1259498

St. Margaret Middle School Library
1716-A Churchville Road
Bel Air, Maryland 21015

The Library of Future Medicine

The Human Genome Project

JAMES TORIELLO

The Rosen Publishing Group, Inc.
New York

Published in 2003 by The Rosen Publishing Group, Inc.
29 East 21st Street, New York, NY 10010

Copyright © 2003 by The Rosen Publishing Group, Inc.

First Edition

All rights reserved. No part of this book may be reproduced in any form without permission in writing from the publisher, except by a reviewer.

Library of Congress Cataloging-in-Publication Data

Toriello, James.
The Human Genome Project / James Toriello.
p. cm.— (The library of future medicine)
Includes bibliographical references and index.
Summary: Describes potential uses for the ten-year, multimillion dollar Human Genome Project and its process of gene mapping.
ISBN 0-8239-3671-6
1. Human Genome Project—Juvenile literature. [1. Human Genome Project. 2. Gene mapping. 3. Medicine. 4. Genetics.] I. Title. II. Series.
QH445.2 .T67 2002
611'.01816—dc21

2001006264

Manufactured in the United States of America

Cover Image: A scientist examines DNA gel as part of a genetic engineering research project.

Contents

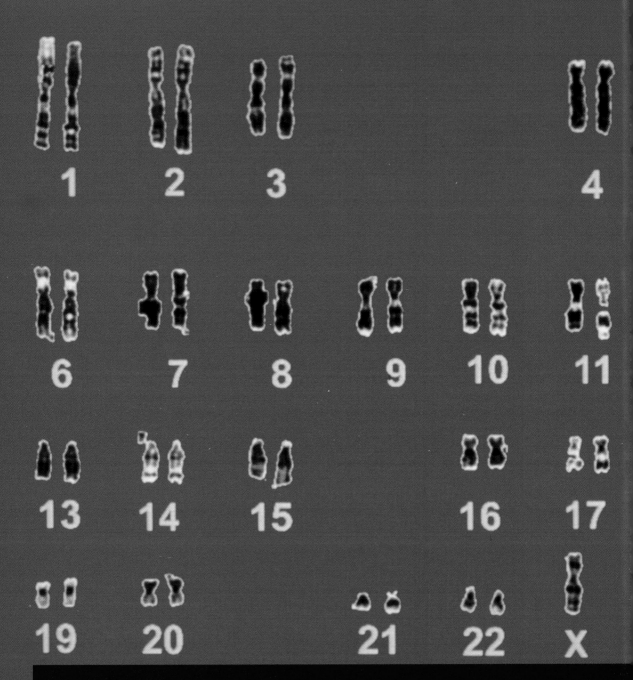

Human chromosomes consist of twenty-two pairs of non-sex chromosomes and one pair of sex chromosomes, labeled XX or XY.

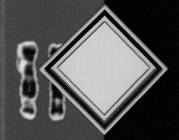

Introduction

Today, scientists and doctors are in the process of preparing another new set of "maps" of the human anatomy. But this is a very unique set of maps. In recent years, new developments in imaging technology, such as CAT (computerized axial tomography) scans, PET (positron emission tomography) scans, and MRIs (magnetic resonance imaging), have given the medical profession new ways to look inside human beings. But what researchers are now trying to unravel is infinitely more ambitious. They are trying to decode the molecular arrangement of the chromosomes in the reproductive cells of the human body. This molecular arrangement is known as the human genome. It is the blueprint for all the physical and behavioral traits that an individual can pass on to his or her offspring. It is the code for building a human being.

Every cell in the human body contains twenty-three pairs of chromosomes. Scientists identify them by number, as when they refer to "chromosome 7." The chromosomes that determine sex are an exception.

They are called the X and Y chromosomes. Females have two X chromosomes; males have an X and a Y chromosome. Each chromosome consists of two long chains of molecules wrapped around each other in a spiral shape known as a double helix. The two strands are connected to each other at many points, making the whole structure look something like a spiral staircase, or a kind of twisted ladder. Each of the connections, or "rungs" of this ladder, is a gene, a molecule that controls one or more human traits, working in complex ways with other genes to determine the kind of person that is created.

During human reproduction, the twenty-three pairs of chromosomes in the nucleus of each parent's germ cell (the egg or sperm cell) separate before the cells

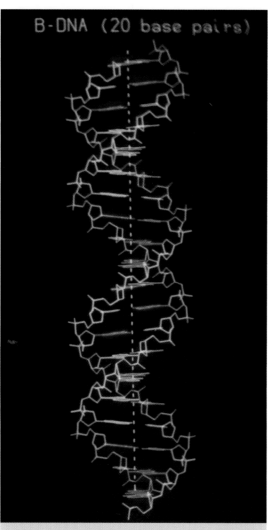

B-DNA (20 base pairs)

The structural arrangement of DNA, commonly described as a double helix, looks like a long ladder that has been twisted into a coil.

reproduce, so these cells have only half the number of chromosomes of normal cells. Then, when a sperm cell unites with an egg cell, the chromosomes pair up again. This means that each parent contributes half of the genes that comprise the genetic code of the offspring. It is through this process of mixing genes that children not only inherit the traits of their parents but become different from both of their parents as a result of the new genetic sequences they inherit.

The thousands of genes on each of these chromosomes govern everything the human body will become. That includes any inherited illnesses, any physical deformities, and any weakness or predisposition to develop or suffer from some disease. It is hoped that an understanding of the human genome will lead to a host of new drugs and therapies for these diseases. In fact, it is hoped that with sufficient technical knowledge it may even be possible, before birth, to alter the genetic code and prevent the appearance of these illnesses. Beyond this, some people have raised the possibility, fraught with ethical difficulties, of producing "designer babies"—children with the qualities their parents desire, such as increased intelligence.

But this genetic revolution did not begin in the 1990s, when scientists first started to map the human genome. It actually started more than a century before, with a humble vegetable many kids won't even eat for dinner—the pea.

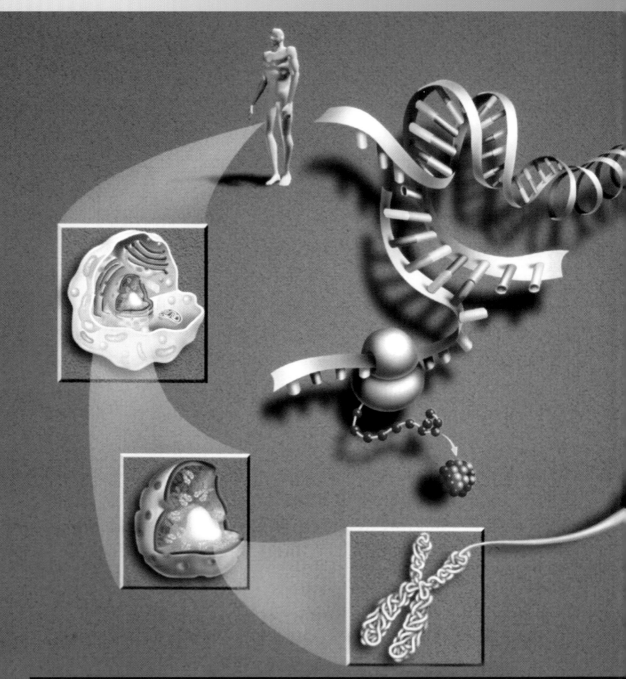

This diagram illustrates how human traits are transferred by genes through the duplication of chromosomes. *Counterclockwise from top*, a human, a cell, the nucleus of a cell, a pair of chromosomes, chromosomes enlarged to show the double helix.

From Wrinkled Peas to DNA

In 1843, an intelligent and practical young man joined an Augustinian monastery at Brünn in what is now the Czech Republic. The monk, eventually ordained a priest, was Father Gregor Johann Mendel. He attended the University of Vienna in 1851 to be trained in the sciences, but he failed an exam that would have let him teach science to others. He had, however, a scientific mind and was intensely curious.

He was also an excellent gardener. In 1857, Mendel began to notice something about the pea plants that he grew in the garden of the monastery. It was not something that hadn't been noticed before. It was, in fact, common knowledge to most farmers. But no one before had thought about it in quite the same way that Mendel did. These pea plants passed on certain traits through their seeds to daughter pea plants from one generation to the next.

Mendel soon began a series of statistical experiments with peas to describe this phenomenon. He used 20,000 plants in one trial alone. He studied traits like the color of the peas, which could be green or yellow, whether the skin of the peas was wrinkled or smooth, and whether the stalks of the plants were long or short. From these experiments and similar ones with fuchsias, corn, and other plants, Mendel discovered that there must be two genetic factors for each of the characteristics he tracked. Most of the time a plant with, say, yellow peas would produce seeds that would grow into more plants with yellow peas. But every now and then a plant with yellow peas might produce an offspring with green peas. It seemed that there were two "tendencies" in each seed, one of which was more frequently dominant than the other, which seemed to be recessive—that is, hidden—or often not manifested in the daughter plants. If it was dominant, the trait would be expressed even if a recessive factor for the opposite trait was present. The pea would be wrinkled, for example. If, however, the trait was recessive, it would appear in a daughter plant only if both factors in the parent plant were for that recessive trait. Mendel noted that these factors did not mix. You could never grow a plant with peas half yellow and half green. One trait always dominated.

Mendel also realized that with sexual reproduction between two parent organisms, each parent contributes one set of genetic factors to the offspring, either a dominant or recessive factor. Mendel worked out a series of diagrams showing how, if one knew the traits of the parents, as well as their parents, it was possible to work out the statistical probability of a certain trait appearing among the offspring. Dominant traits would appear more frequently, but if a recessive trait was present in one or both of the parents or ancestors of the parents, that recessive trait would appear in a predictable number of offspring.

Today, we know that these genetic factors, dominant or recessive, reside in the genes that make up the chromosomes. Mendel's statistical laws are today the foundation of the modern science of genetics. At the time, however, the discoveries were mostly ignored. Mendel published details of his work and sent letters about it to prominent scientists, but his work was forgotten until 1900.

DNA

Today, we know that the factors Mendel thought determined inherited traits are genes, the molecular units that hold together the long chains of the chromosome molecules. The long strands of molecules making up the chromosome itself have been given a name: deoxyribonucleic acid, or DNA. DNA was discovered around 1869 by the Swiss doctor Friedrich Miescher, who analyzed the bandages of soldiers in a small German town named Tübingen near Stuttgart. He found the DNA molecule in the pus of their wounds and later guessed that it would prove to be an "alphabet" of hereditary characteristics. Even so, the molecule remained a mystery until 1953. In that year, Francis Crick and James Watson finally discovered the unique chemical structure of DNA, the spiral winding of the two strands and the chemistry of the connecting rungs. Their discovery earned them the Nobel Prize in 1962.

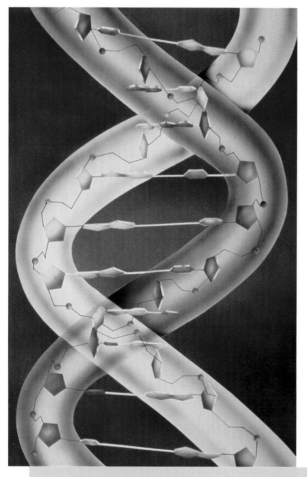

The DNA molecule is an extremely long and complex double helix of tightly ordered atoms. The connections between the two strands, the "steps" of this ladderlike structure, are very special, since they can only be constructed of one of four substances: adenine, guanine, thymine, or cytosine.

The two strands of the DNA molecule are connected at various points by one of four substances (adenine, guanine, thymine, or cytosine), thereby giving DNA its ladderlike structure.

James Watson *(left)* and Francis Crick won the Nobel Prize for medicine in 1962 for cracking the DNA code.

This special structure makes DNA a genetic code. The cells of the body, each of which has a set of DNA chromosomes in its nucleus, can use this code to create certain amino acids, which are then combined to make proteins and enzymes. Proteins are the basic building materials of human tissues. Enzymes facilitate chemical reactions.

Twenty amino acids make up all the proteins and enzymes in the human body. The creation of each amino acid is triggered by a different combination (or sequential order) of three of the four basic substances that make up each gene of the DNA molecule. The four substances are identified by the first letter of their names. For example, the combination CAG (cytosine, adenine, guanine) will produce a specific amino acid.

RNA, or ribonucleic acid, is another long chain molecule very similar to DNA, except that it uses a substance known as uracil instead of thymine in its rungs. Some strands of RNA act as messengers. Called messenger RNA or mRNA, they transfer the code from DNA to special cell structures known as ribosomes. The ribosomes create amino acids and string them together to make proteins.

Human beings have about 40,000 genes on their chromosomes. The precise number is still uncertain. The vast majority of these genes are shared with other species, like apes, mice, and fish, which reflects our evolutionary heritage. Only a relatively small number of these genes are unique to human beings. Furthermore, scientists believe that the majority of our genetic sequences are "junk" or "noise"— that is, they have no function. Some may be the remnants of traits that humans no longer exhibit. Some may have a yet unknown function in helping other genes to copy themselves correctly during reproduction. This is one of many areas that must be studied further.

Each gene consists of what is called a base pair, a sequence of two of the four basic substances (cytosine, adenine, guanine, thymine) that forms a chemical connection between the two long, spiral DNA strands. Thousands of these connections, each a different combination of the four substances, run along the DNA strands, holding them together and containing the sequence of instructions for producing an organism. When the two strands of the chromosome pull apart during the reproductive cycle, the base pairs split apart. Using chemicals in the germ cells, they can reform in exactly the same sequence of coded instructions.

THE HUMAN GENOME PROJECT

Because DNA contains the entire blueprint for the human body, scientists reasoned that decoding it all would help them to understand how human organisms work. The first gene was decoded in 1975 from the DNA of a virus. Two years later, a human gene that created a blood protein was isolated.

In the 1990s, the U.S. government sponsored a project to decode the sequence of genes for all of the human genome by issuing grants and funding research programs. The project was coordinated through the National Institutes of Health and the Department of Energy, and involves scientists from England and elsewhere in the world as well as the United States.

The methods for studying genes have changed over the years. The English chemist Frederick Sanger invented the

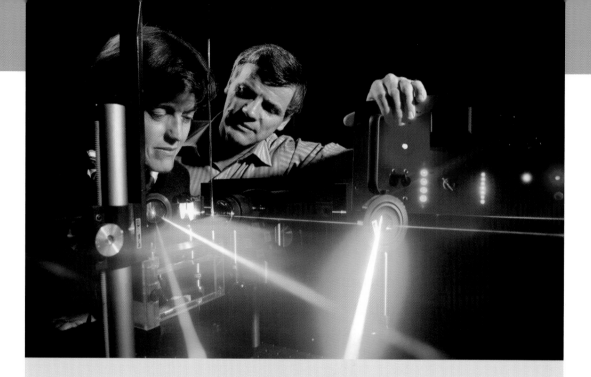

Biologists at the California Institute of Technology demonstrate a machine that uses lasers to read DNA sequences.

chain termination method as a way to decode DNA in the 1960s. In the 1980s, Michael Hunkapiller, along with Leroy Hood and other scientists and engineers at Applied Biosystems, perfected a new method using fluorescent dyes to locate genes that made sequencing much faster. Scientists first worked with the DNA of simpler organisms like bacteria to determine if their sequencing methods worked properly. They found recurring strands of gene sequences, called transposons, that were like the repeated phrases in a coded message that could be used to help decode it. In the 1990s, James Weber and Gene Myers theorized that large statistical samples could be used in what came to be called a "shotgun approach" to researching the genome. Rather than concentrating on a single small section of DNA at a time, computers allowed researchers to match sequences from all the genes at once. Highly controversial at first, the technique was championed by Craig Venter.

While Venter started out as part of the Human Genome Project, he eventually split with the federally sponsored research group. Part of the conflict concerned the question of how the information about genes should be used. Some scientists believed that it should be shared freely. Others, including Venter, thought that the process should be more like a commercial enterprise. Venter eventually formed a private company to decode the human genome. Today, the company is called Celera Genomics. A competition began between Celera and the government-sponsored scientists to be the first to fully sequence the human genome.

On June 26, 2000, both the government-sponsored researchers and Celera announced that the majority of the work was complete. Approximately 95 percent of the human genome had been sequenced, with an accuracy of 99.9 percent. The project had been planned to take about fifteen years, but rapid advances in biotechnology brought the project close to completion much more rapidly. But many scientists

The headquarters of Celera Genomics in Rockville, Maryland. Celera Genomics, along with the Human Genome Project, announced a rough-draft sequence of the human genome in June 2000.

pointed out that it was too soon to celebrate. The two groups had finished only a rough draft and weren't even sure precisely how many genes humans have. Some parts of the genome had not been verified, or "proofread."

Scientists expect to have a final version of the human genome by 2003. But even then, the work will have just begun. Knowing the molecular sequences—the order of the genes—is not the same thing as knowing what each gene does or what trait it is responsible for. That requires a much more complex investigative process, involving, among other things, the elimination of those sequences that are just "noise." And until we know which molecular sequence is responsible for a particular trait, we cannot design drugs to reverse the effects of genetically caused diseases or deformities.

With the exact chemical sequence of human DNA now being worked out, it will be necessary to note the presence or absence of particular genes or combinations of genes in individuals who have certain traits or suffer from certain illnesses. When this is done for each gene, we will finally know the secret of how human beings are constructed.

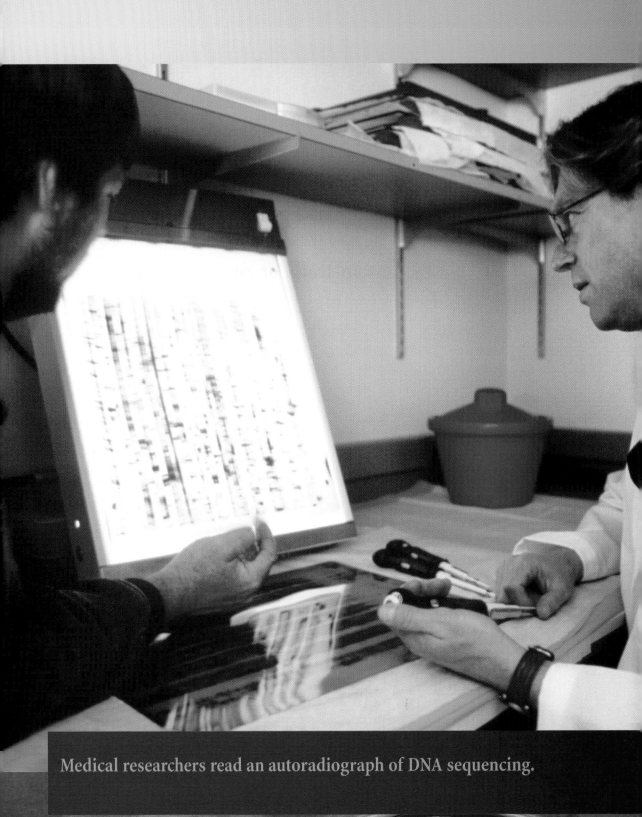

Medical researchers read an autoradiograph of DNA sequencing.

2 ◇ Testing

Thyroid cancer is a relatively rare disease. The first people to study it eventually realized that it was actually four different types of cancer, each of which affected different cells in different ways. By analyzing many patients, they realized that one type of thyroid cancer ran in families. Members of the same family often got the disease, even though their environments were different. This meant that the disease was probably inherited. If so, one or more genes must be involved. Scientists then began to look for "genetic markers," or common genes that could be found in everyone with the disease. Once they found a marker, they prepared a test that could always find it.

Genetic testing, or genetic screening, first became common during the 1980s. The tests now cover a wide range of medical conditions and are performed at various stages of a person's life. In the future, such tests will become more routine.

Having a gene that is a marker for a disease doesn't mean that you will get the disease. And even though scientists may be able to link a gene to a specific ailment, in most cases they are not exactly sure what the connection is. But finding that connection often allows scientists and doctors to help people before the disease strikes.

MUTATIONS

Scientists believe that many genetic illnesses are caused by a mutation in the genetic alphabet that is passed from generation to generation. A mutation is a random change in the molecular sequence of the genes that alters the coded instructions for making a human being. Mutations can occur when DNA molecules copy themselves but make mistakes during the copying process.

There are several reasons mutations occur. Radiation, for example, can destroy or break the links in the DNA molecule. Diseases themselves play an important role in many mutations. A mutation that helps people survive typhus, for example, would mean that more people with that mutation would survive the disease. That mutation would be passed on from generation to generation. Of course, while it helps people fight typhus, it might hurt in other ways. For example, many African Americans today have sickle-cell anemia, a condition that causes blood cells to collapse. This is a potentially fatal disease. Scientists think it came about because of a mutation that helped people combat malaria.

In the history of evolution, most mutations are dead ends. That is, they produce organisms that are so abnormal that they cannot survive. A small number of mutations produce beneficial traits, characteristics that improve the chances of an organism's survival in a particular environment. These mutations are responsible for the changes we see in living creatures over long periods of time. Still other mutations, the ones we are concerned with here, produce illnesses and abnormalities that are not initially lethal and that can be passed on to the next generation before the parent is stricken.

OTHER TESTS

In the procedure known as amniocentesis, doctors poke a long needle into a pregnant woman's abdomen to sample the amniotic fluid around the fetus. Cells from the fetus are then analyzed. The test looks for common abnormalities that could lead to Down's syndrome or other severe developmental maladies.

In some cases, parents rely on the test results to decide whether to abort a fetus. Amniocentesis became common in the 1990s, especially for older mothers whose children are at greater risk. But the test is extremely invasive, and safer methods are being developed. It is now possible to learn a great deal about a fetus by sampling the mother's blood, and further advances are expected soon.

By 2000, there were approximately 200 genetic tests for diseases linked to single genes or chromosomes. These include Down's syndrome, phenylketonuria (PKU), Huntington's disease, myotonic dystrophy, and fragile X syndrome. More tests are being developed. In some cases, however, tests may not find everyone with the disease. For example, just under 70 percent of the people suffering from cystic fibrosis share a genetic mutation of a gene on chromosome 7. Searching for just that mutation will not find all people likely to get the disease, just most of them. In these situations, other factors, including other genes and the environment, are involved.

THE FUTURE OF GENETIC TESTING

Genes by themselves do not cause all or even most diseases. But genes do play a role in many situations. Future genetic tests will be aimed at telling people what diseases they are most vulnerable to. It may also tell them how to best avoid these problems.

One of the most important tests that researchers are trying to develop is for Alzheimer's disease. This debilitating

Blueprints and Codes

We often use metaphors to talk about the role that DNA, genes, and chromosomes play in human development. One popular metaphor compares genes to blueprints. This is appropriate because genes lay out the basic design of cells and organs. However, looking at genes is not quite like looking at a blueprint. A blueprint, for example, can be a drawing of a house. Genes, however, are a code that must be translated into amino acids. These in turn act and react in different ways to build and manage our bodies.

You cannot look at a chromosome and see right away what a human being is supposed to look like. The DNA code was not designed for human interpretation, like the blueprint of a house. So the task of figuring out which pieces of code are responsible for particular human traits is very difficult.

and fatal disease harms its victims, generally elderly, by killing brain cells. The disease degrades their ability to remember things and think clearly.

There are three varieties of the genes that predispose someone to suffer from Alzheimer's disease. They are called apolipoprotein genes. The differences between the three versions of these genes alter the type of protein that the genes

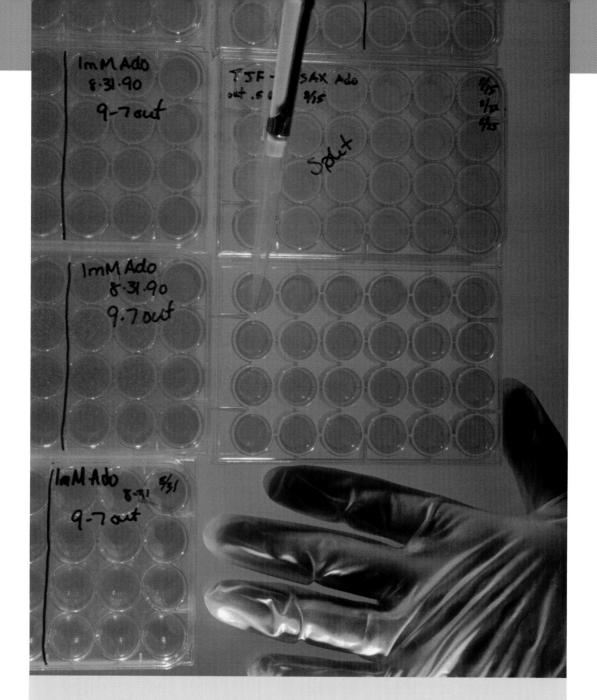

A researcher prepares culture dishes of human T cells for DNA transfer therapy.

produce. That slight difference is somehow enough to encourage the disease, though scientists do not yet understand why. Someone with one such gene has a 47 percent chance of developing the disease. Someone with two of these genes has a 91 percent chance of developing Alzheimer's.

By screening people for these genes, doctors can now recommend drugs that will alleviate some early Alzheimer's symptoms. They can also recommend nutritional programs that may be of help. Families who know that Alzheimer's is a possibility can also be better prepared to deal with it.

One of the Alzheimer's genes has also been linked to another ailment, coronary heart disease. This gene creates a protein that affects the body's ability to process cholesterol, a specific kind of fat that blocks coronary arteries. With heart disease the top cause of death in the United States, scientists are studying this gene carefully to see if it may reveal ways of preventing the disease.

DRUGS

Besides predicting whether people will get a disease, doctors in the future may use genetic profiles to select what drug to treat them with when they get it. A new branch of medicine called pharmacogenetics has been established to study the different interactions between drugs and genetic conditions. Even common ailments such as the flu may attack people differently depending on their genetic makeup.

Some scientists predict that the creation of genetic profiles for each person will become routine in the future. These profiles will supply doctors with a great deal of information about an individual's susceptibility to certain illnesses and his or her reaction to certain therapies.

BEYOND DISEASE

Eventually, genetic testing may go beyond treating illnesses. By knowing which proteins the body can make efficiently, it is possible that doctors will be able to recommend diets and exercise routines that will maximize a person's health. Athletes might be encouraged to eat certain foods for peak performance. "Brain food" might be on the school lunch menu the week before finals, with different choices for different genetic types.

While genetic testing is a powerful tool, some people worry that it could be abused. For example, insurance companies might deny health insurance to people with genes linked to certain diseases. Or employers might not hire people with genes linked to undesirable behaviors, or even independent thinking. And some people criticize prenatal screening that leads to abortion. Anyone in possession of a person's precise genetic code has a great deal of information about that person, and the potential for abuse is great.

The ethics of screening are still being debated. In the meantime, we must remember that, except for some rare ailments, genes do not imply destiny. A genetic predisposition to get a disease works in conjunction with other factors, such as environment, diet, and behavior. A gene may be recessive and not manifest itself for several generations. There is no reason to suppose that the diagnosis of a genetic defect means that an individual will suffer from some disease. Realistically, however, the chances of getting that disease increase. Would people want to have that kind of information about themselves? It is not an easy question to answer, particularly when there is no therapy or cure for the condition.

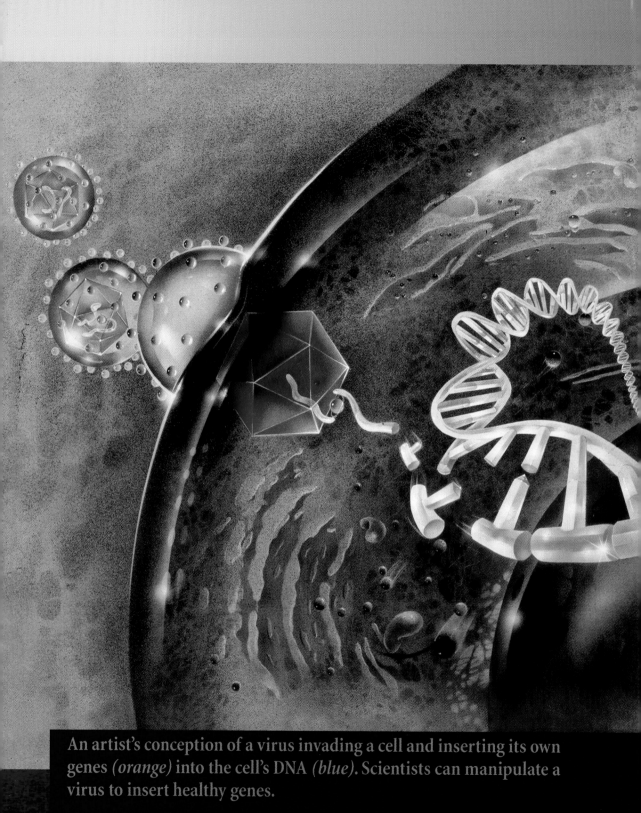

An artist's conception of a virus invading a cell and inserting its own genes *(orange)* into the cell's DNA *(blue)*. Scientists can manipulate a virus to insert healthy genes.

3 › Gene Therapy

A small number of children in the 1980s and 1990s actually lived in germ-free plastic bubbles. It was the only way that doctors could think of to protect them. These children had a rare disease called severe combined immune deficiency (SCID), or adenosine deaminase deficiency (ADA).

SCID is caused by a mutation in the gene deoxyadenosine that depletes the body's supply of T cells. T cells are special white blood cells that destroy bacteria and viruses. When we get a cold, the T cells go to work. If they weren't there to do the job, we would get extremely sick and could die. In a healthy person, a liter of blood contains about 400,000 white blood cells. Most of these are T cells. Someone with SCID might have no more than 750 T cells or even less per half-liter of blood.

Doctors fought SCID in a variety of ways. At first, they developed a drug called PEG-ADA. It took over for the malfunctioning gene and prompted the body's cells to make the protein they needed to construct more T cells. Unfortunately, this synthesized protein caused allergic reactions in some people. Even for the people it helped, the drug's effects were only temporary. Patients needed an injection of the expensive medicine every month.

Knowing the genetic cause of SCID led researchers to believe that they might cure the disease by replacing the "bad" sequence of DNA with a good one. They decided to use a special type of virus called a retrovirus. Viruses are very primitive organisms, little more than bundles of DNA themselves. In nature, retroviruses enter the nuclei of cells and insert their genetic code into the DNA of the host cell so that they can reproduce themselves. In the laboratory, these viruses can be used to change the DNA sequences of various cells. Once the cells are "fixed," they would be encouraged to reproduce before being returned to the patient, so that healthy cells would replace the defective ones.

Doctors French Anderson, Michael Blaese, and Steven Rosenberg led the effort to cure SCID with gene therapy. On September 14, 1990, Anderson and Blaese treated a three-year-old girl named Ashanthi DeSilva with their new procedure. Within a year, her T cell count rose to 1,600 cells per liter of blood, about two and a half times her count before gene therapy began. It was still a far cry from normal, but it greatly improved her condition.

STEM CELLS

Gene therapy was merely one step in the long fight against SCID. Altered T cells cannot live forever. Eventually they die and have to be replaced. A true cure for the disease would alter the cells that produce the body's T cells. Then the body could produce more of its own T cells. These parent cells are known as stem cells. They became the focus of the next stage of gene therapy. Stem cells are young, unspecialized cells that, depending on how they are stimulated, can grow into other types of cells. They are found in human embryos and in a few areas of the adult human body.

The stem cells responsible for forming T cells had been studied for a number of reasons unrelated to SCID, but those studies gave scientists a lot of data to work with. On May 13, 1993, a team led by Dr. Anderson collected seven liters of blood from a patient and began the process of seeding the blood with stem cells that would turn into T cells. They returned the gene-altered stem cells to the patient's body and waited. Unfortunately, the experiment failed. Still, the basic concept and procedures may lead to future successes.

OTHER APPROACHES

The early work on SCID genes demonstrated the basic paths that gene therapy is likely to take in the future. Replacing "bad"

DNA and Forensic Medicine

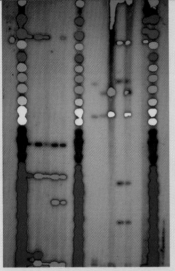

DNA fingerprinting

Doctors aren't the only ones who use genetic testing to help them do their work. Detectives do, too. DNA testing allows detectives to match DNA found at a crime scene with a suspect's own DNA. This is called DNA fingerprinting.

DNA often deteriorates as time passes. And it is not always possible to obtain complete samples of DNA from a crime scene. Testing methods currently in use rely on statistical averages, and there is a margin for error. Current methods are better at ruling out matches than positively identifying suspects. It sounds very good to hear that there is a 99.9 percent chance that there is a match between DNA samples, but what this means is that if 10,000 individuals are tested, there will be 10 mismatches. Or 100 mismatches in a sampling of 100,000 individuals. That is a significant number. Would you want to risk your freedom with those odds? For all these reasons, DNA fingerprinting remains controversial.

As methods improve, DNA fingerprinting may become quite common. It's possible that it will be used for identification and security purposes. At present, however, it is too expensive and time-consuming for routine use.

genes with "good" genes directly by altering the DNA of the body's cells may provide a cure for a disease. Scientists have already replaced as much as a third of a human liver with tissue that has been altered to fight a disease known as familial hypercholesterolemia. In this disease, the patients' liver cells lack a gene that allows them to remove cholesterol from the blood. High levels of cholesterol can cause heart disease and death.

At present, doctors must remove the tissue to perform this type of therapy. Whether it uses blood, bone marrow, or even a part of a liver, such a procedure can be lengthy, costly, and even life threatening. Scientists are working on techniques that would allow them to target parts of the body with a simple injection, which eliminates the need to surgically remove tissue. This sort of system might cure a disease such as Duchenne's muscular dystrophy, which affects certain muscles in men, by sending new DNA material to the body's vast network of muscles.

Researchers are studying a similar method to cure cystic fibrosis, an inherited disease that damages the lungs and pancreas. Cystic fibrosis attacks about 35,000 people, mostly children, every year. It generally kills its victims before they reach the age of forty. The large size of the gene responsible for cystic fibrosis and the fact that the cells to be targeted are in the lungs led scientists to develop a unique method to engineer a genetic change. They used a new type of virus, called an adenovirus, to insert new DNA into cells. While

GM Foods

A field worker checks genetically modified corn in a greenhouse at DeKalb Genetics Corp. in Mystic, Connecticut.

The benefits that will come to people from a comprehensive knowledge of the genetic structure of organisms will be much broader than new medicines and therapies. Extensive research into the genomes of plants is beginning to produce foods with new characteristics. Through genetic engineering, scientists have created corn plants that contain their own pesticides, tomatoes that stay fresher longer, and varieties of basic cereal grains that are more nutritious. Such products are known as genetically modified, or GM, foods.

Such products are controversial, however. Will private, for-profit developers investigate the potential health risks from genetically modified foods carefully enough? Will such products be developed because they are better for people or because they are more convenient or profitable for their manufacturers?

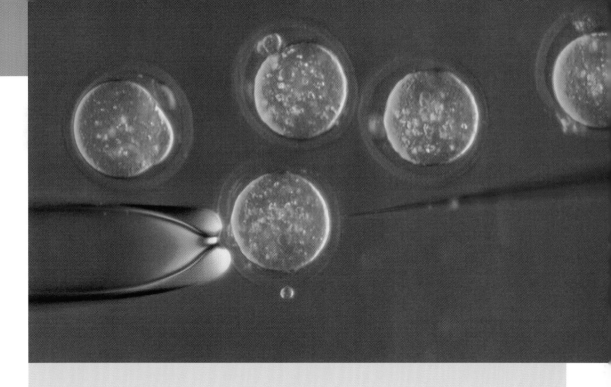

Foreign DNA can be introduced into a cell to change the cell's genetic makeup.

early tests in animals seemed to work, scientists ran into several problems with humans. In some cases, the person's immune system treated these new cells as foreign bodies and attacked them. Still, successful gene therapy for cystic fibrosis seems likely within the next decade.

ORGAN TRANSPLANTS

Stem cells may also someday be used as seeds to grow new organs. Organ transplants have become an important part of medical treatment in the last twenty years. However, such procedures are hampered by the body's immune system, its

Animal Testing

Carpenters have a variety of tools available to them as they build houses—hammers, saws, drills, and so on. Genetic researchers and doctors have tools as well. Their tools are specialized for working with DNA.

"Knockout mice" aren't mice trained to fight in the boxing ring. They are mice that have been bred for genetic research. Scientists have "knocked out," or deleted, an important gene or DNA sequence in their chromosomes so that they can observe the effects on the mice.

Animals, insects, and plants have long been used in a variety of genetic experiments. This testing can go far beyond the type of experiments that Gregor Mendel did with peas. For example, the ability of mice to learn simple tasks makes them suitable for experiments dealing with different brain functions. Of course, scientists must be careful not to jump to conclusions about humans based simply on experiments with other creatures.

natural defense against invading microorganisms. Special immunosuppressive drugs must be used to keep the body from attacking the transplanted organ. In theory, an organ grown from the body's own stem cells won't produce such an immune reaction. If such organs can be grown under laboratory conditions from stem cells with healthy DNA, it may become possible to replace genetically damaged tissues with entirely new, healthy organs.

BIOCHEMICAL PRODUCTION

Gene therapy, or the direct replacement of segments of DNA material in cells, is already being used to create chemicals and medicines. People who suffer from diabetes, for example, are unable to manufacture a hormone called insulin, which helps to metabolize sugar. To keep themselves healthy, people who suffer from this disease, which is inherited, must receive regular treatments of insulin. In 1981, scientists learned how to insert the human genes that make insulin into the common bacteria *Escherichia coli*. The bacteria then become insulin farms, producing human insulin that now helps to save many people's lives. Other hormones, including human growth hormone, are now made this way.

The process of using recombinant DNA to grow synthetic substances is also being used to create vaccines, such as the vaccine for hepatitis. Hemophiliacs, whose blood lacks a clotting factor and who cannot stop bleeding when injured, control their disease with artificial blood clotting factors made the same way. A wide variety of similar medicines, artificial hormones, and vaccines are currently being developed.

An artist's conception of a portion of the network of neurons, or nerve cells, within the human brain

Genetics and the Mind

Most of the diseases that affect the mind are complex. Often there are no laboratory tests that can show a doctor precisely what the problem is. The symptoms can be complicated and confusing. This complexity makes it more difficult to treat mental illness. While doctors have a lot of experience and success with certain types of mental disease, researchers are working feverishly to provide more basic information about the brain in general. The science of genetics is playing an important role.

HUNTINGTON'S DISEASE

Some mental disorders can be linked fairly closely to genetic abnormalities. Huntington's disease is one example. This disease begins with a loss of mental faculties such as memory. Gradually, a victim begins to see things that aren't there and believe things that are obviously false to others.

The disease has been traced through two family groups that have passed it down unknowingly from generation to generation. Scientists therefore believe that it is caused by a genetic defect and that genetic mutations can cause it in other families. Doctors learned about the genetic connection in the 1980s. At this moment, they have no cure. Testing can, however, help identify the ailment. Further research may someday suggest a cure, either through gene therapy or special drugs.

SCHIZOPHRENIA

Because it is caused by one gene, Huntington's disease is considered exceptional. Scientists believe that most mental illnesses have several causes, including social and environmental factors. Perhaps no illness demonstrates the complex relationship between mind and body better than schizophrenia.

Schizophrenia is a terrifying disease that usually strikes young adults and older teenagers. It causes a wide range of mental problems, from an inability to focus attention to bizarre hallucinations. A person suffering from schizophrenia can be said to be literally losing his or her mind.

Scientists believe that several genes working together help to create the conditions for this disease. They also suspect that these genes may be different in different individuals. But there are also other factors involved. Psychological stress and trauma can trigger a disease if the right genes are there, but the disease might not appear at all without such a trigger.

Unraveling exactly which genes are involved and how they interact may help doctors fight the disease in several ways in the future. For example, new medicines have been developed in the past two decades to help cope with schizophrenia. Certain medicines work better for some people than others. At the moment, doctors select the drugs based on their experience and trial and error. There is hope, however, that further study of brain chemistry and perhaps genetics can lead to better prescriptions.

ALZHEIMER'S AND OTHER DISEASES

A strong genetic link between a gene on chromosome 19 and Alzheimer's disease was discovered in the 1990s. However, scientists have also learned that genes on two other chromosomes may play a role in some cases. By studying the disease, they were led to investigate specific proteins that were produced by the suspect genes. The role that these proteins play in causing the disease, which is currently incurable, is being investigated.

A lab technician tests tissue cell cultures for a protein linked to Alzheimer's disease and related brain disorders.

EATING DISORDERS

Recent research has shown that, for some people, obesity can be caused or encouraged by a person's genetic makeup. In some cases, a person's thyroid gland makes him or her gain weight almost no matter how little that person eats or how much he or she diets. Some people are "programmed" by nature to want certain fatty foods. Fighting this programming is extremely hard. Disorders such as anorexia nervosa will also probably benefit from research at the genetic level.

 ## How Evolution Works

People tend to think of the process of evolution as one of endless improvement in the way that the human organism functions. But in truth the process of evolution has a very narrow goal—increasing reproductive success. Here's an example of what that means.

Heart disease is one of the leading killers of people today. Will we ever evolve hearts that are stronger and less vulnerable to failure? Probably not, because there is no evolutionary pressure to do so. Most people who suffer from heart disease do not become sick or experience coronary failure until their forties or fifties or later, well after the years in which they have children. So the genetic triggers for heart disease are passed on before they die. Through the artificial manipulation of genes, we may one day improve the functioning of our hearts, but natural selection cannot do this, unless a mutation producing a stronger heart has other survival benefits.

GENES FOR INTELLIGENCE

There is no gene that makes one person smarter than another. The very notion of intelligence, in any case, is not easily definable in biological terms. People who think that the science of genetics will in the future permit the design of intelligent children fail to take into account all the other factors that determine intelligence—proper nurturing and exposure to the right intellectual stimuli among them.

One has to be very careful about identifying real biological traits before discussing inherited characteristics. One person's notion of "smartness" might not impress another person at all. Is intelligence the ability to talk with sophistication about ideas absorbed from books, quickly solve a jigsaw puzzle or a complex mathematical equation, or properly respond in a social situation with a witty remark? It is unlikely that genes alone control such complex forms of behavior.

That does not mean, however, that genes don't play a role in intelligence. All the genes that together determine the characteristics, growth rates, and healthy functioning of brain tissue are sure to have an effect on the intellectual abilities of an individual. But it is next to impossible to classify people genetically as more "smart" or less "smart." A person with all the right genes, if such genes could be identified, might be born under circumstances that limit his or her educational opportunities, and the "smartness" might never manifest itself.

The Tree of Life

In addition to medical benefits, the science of genetics promises to teach us a great deal about the evolutionary history of living creatures. In the past, scientists depended upon comparative anatomy to determine which organisms descended from which other organisms. They would decide, for example, that the bones of one animal so closely resembled the bones of an earlier animal that the later animal must have evolved from the earlier.

This method has proved very valuable in ordering the tree of life, but it is somewhat subjective and mistakes have been made. Much more accurate is comparing sequences of genetic code in the DNA of the two creatures, if samples can be obtained. So far, scientists have obtained complete genomes for the bacterium *Escherichia coli*, the common fruit fly, and the common roundworm, and progress is being made on the genome of the laboratory mouse. As the genetic sequences of more and more organisms become known to us, we will have a better idea of how related we are to various creatures and from which ones we have evolved.

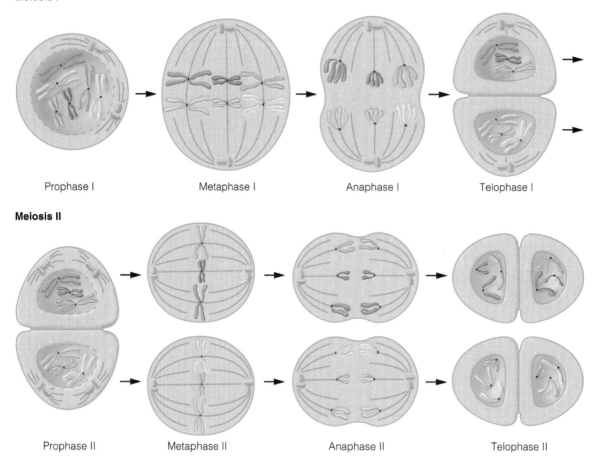

An artist's conception of meiosis, the process of cell division that prepares germ cells for reproduction

5   Genetic Engineering

There are some human traits or abnormalities that have a clear and precise relationship to specific genes. Down's syndrome, for example, occurs when a person has an extra copy of chromosome 21. Presently, hundreds of thousands of women and their fetuses undergo genetic testing for such conditions every year. In some cases, fetuses with problems are aborted, a type of genetic selection that is legal but also controversial.

Not all genetic screening is controversial, however, and in most cases it clearly enhances lives. One test for newborns, for example, looks for a condition known as phenylketonuria (PKU). Children who have it are put on a special diet that allows them to develop normally.

Screening can also take place before a couple decides to marry or have children. Some Jewish communities in the United States use genetic screening for Tay-Sachs disease. Two people with genes for the

Cancer

A fermentation tank that breeds yeast cells, whose DNA will be used to create a vaccine for liver cancer

Cancer has become a leading cause of death in the Western world over the past century, even as doctors work hard to fight it. In America, it accounts for about one out of every five deaths. Scientists believe there are many causes for cancer. One may be pollution and another may be the general increase in background radiation. But researchers also believe that many cancers may be triggered by genes.

The full list of cancers could fill several pages of this book. Among the biggest killers in America is lung cancer. While there are other factors involved, cigarette smoking is by far the biggest cause of this type of cancer. Experts believe most people can avoid it by simply not smoking.

Other widespread cancers include skin cancer and prostate cancer. Most cancers don't show up until people reach middle age or older. Several early screening tests are now available to help catch cancer in its early stages. Besides genetic tests, these include physical exams, ultrasound, and radioisotope scanning.

disease, which is recessive, would have a one-in-four chance of having a baby with the disease. They would be strongly counseled against marrying.

The moral and ethical concerns involved in genetic screening will undoubtedly be debated for some time to come. Do we have the right to know our genetic makeup, or to judge people, categorize them, and decide their futures based on our knowledge of their genetic inheritance? But genetic

 ## Studying DNA

Changing the DNA in the nucleus of a cell is not as easy as changing the paneling in a house. Scientists often rely on a special type of virus to do the job. Called a retrovirus, this virus unravels the DNA strands in the nucleus and then inserts the code for its own reproduction into the DNA sequence. When the DNA subdivides later on, this code is passed on. If the work is done in a germ cell, the new code will be passed on to children.

One of the most useful methods of studying inheritance doesn't actually examine DNA itself. Studies of identical twins compare the characteristics of genetically similar individuals raised in both the same environment and different environments. These studies have been used to show the influence of genes and environment on certain characteristics, including behavior.

Test-Tube Babies

The urge to reproduce is programmed into all creatures. So it was inevitable that mankind would turn to science to help with reproductive problems.

Fertility medicine is devoted to helping people have babies. A range of different drugs can be used to enhance fertility or improve the odds of having a baby. In very special cases, the only way to have a baby is by artificial insemination. Eggs are removed from a woman's ovaries, fertilized with special tools in a lab, and then returned to her body. The children who are produced through this method are sometimes called test-tube babies, but they actually develop within their mothers' wombs like all children.

science has the potential to go beyond simple screening. Scientists have already isolated many genes in different species and changed them. From a technical perspective, making these changes in a human germ cell—a sperm or egg cell—is not that much more difficult.

This is genetic engineering, and it is by far the most controversial aspect of gene science today. Many people believe that altering the genes passed on to our children and our children's children is a sin. Even though the intention is good, they say, the result may not be predictable.

The human body is extremely complex. It seems unlikely that scientists will be able to use genetic engineering to make a supersmart or superathletic human in the near future. It is very possible, however, that biotechnology will allow mankind to wipe out certain diseases through genetic engineering and in vitro fertilization within the next two decades.

Genetic science is still in its early stages. Scientists are still learning how to put their discoveries to use. This new dictionary of human life known as the human genome will undoubtedly lead to incredible discoveries in the future. Doctors in the late twenty-first century may shake their heads in amazement when they learn that their ancestors didn't even know what the genes in their bodies were, let alone what each one did.

Glossary

adenine   One of the chemical bases in DNA and RNA. This molecule always combines with thymine in DNA or uracil in RNA.

amino acids   The basic building blocks of proteins. Proteins perform a wide variety of functions in organisms. DNA and RNA use amino acids to construct or regulate proteins and thus guide cell functions. There are twenty amino acids in the human body.

cell   The smallest living biological unit. In general, cells contain a membrane to separate them from other cells, a nucleus to store genetic material, and cytoplasm, where other cell components are located.

chromosomes   The strands of DNA in each cell that contain hereditary material. In humans, each cell nucleus ordinarily contains twenty-three chromosomes.

cytosine   One of the chemical bases in DNA and RNA. This molecule always combines with guanine.

DNA   Deoxyribonucleic acid; the basic material of genes and chromosomes.

dominant traits Traits that are passed on from generation to generation in genes. A dominant trait will always manifest itself, even if only one gene for it is present.

gene The part of a chromosome that contains genetic instructions used by the cell. Genes create sequences of amino acids, which in turn are built into proteins. These proteins govern cell functions and interact with their surrounding environment.

genetic engineering Altering the characteristics of an organism by changing its genes. Humans have practiced a type of genetic engineering on plants and domestic animals for centuries by selecting those organisms with desirable features for reproduction.

genome The term for an organism's DNA sequences.

germ cell An egg or sperm cell. Unlike other cells, these contain only one set of chromosomes.

guanine One of the chemical bases in DNA and RNA. This molecule always combines with cytosine.

marker A sequence in the DNA code that scientists can search for. Often this is a gene that is somehow connected to an inherited disease or characteristic.

mutation A change in the DNA sequence, or a "mistake" in the genetic code, that alters inherited characteristics.

protein A basic substance used by cells for building new tissue and producing essential biochemicals.

recessive traits Traits that remain "hidden" in offspring unless both genes for the trait are present in the chromosomes.

RNA   Ribonucleic acid; a single strand of nucleic acid. RNA assists in copying the DNA code during reproduction. Messenger RNA transmits instructions from DNA in the nucleus of a cell to a ribosome where protein is created.

thymine   One of the chemical bases in DNA and RNA. This molecule always combines with adenine in DNA.

uracil   One of the chemical bases in RNA. This molecule always combines with adenine.

virus   A microorganism that consists of a protein skin wrapped around a piece of nucleic acid. Common viruses are responsible for diseases such as the flu. Some viruses, however, are used by scientists to alter genes for research and therapy.

For More Information

ORGANIZATIONS

The Hereditary Disease Foundation
130 Pico Boulevard
Santa Monica, CA 90405-1553
(310) 450-9913
Web site: http://www.hdfoundation.org

Human Genome Project Information
Oak Ridge National Laboratory
1060 Commerce Park MS 6480
Oak Ridge, TN 37830
(865) 576-6669
Web site: http://www.ornl.gov/hgmis

The March of Dimes
1275 Mamaroneck Avenue
White Plains, NY 10605
(888) MODIMES (663-4637)
Web site: http://www.modimes.org

WEB SITES

Due to the changing nature of Internet links, the Rosen Publishing Group, Inc., has developed an online list of Web sites related to the subject of this book. This site is updated regularly. Please use this link to access the list:

http://www.rosenlinks.com/lfm/hugp/

For Further Reading

Aronson, Billy. *They Came from DNA*. New York: Scientific American Books for Young Readers, 1993.

Beshore, George. *Sickle Cell Anemia*. New York: Franklin Watts, 1994.

Casanellas, Antonio. *Great Discoveries and Inventions That Improved Human Health*. Milwaukee, WI: Gareth Stevens, 2000.

Darling, David. *The Health Revolution: Surgery and Medicine in the 21st Century*. Parsippany, NJ: Dillon Press, 1996.

Forsyth, Elizabeth H. *The Disease Book: A Kid's Guide*. New York: Walker & Co., 1997.

Frankel, Dr. Edward. *DNA: The Ladder of Life*. New York: McGraw-Hill, 1978.

Hawkes, Nigel. *Medicine and Health*. New York: Twenty-First Century Books, 1994.

O'Neill, Terry, ed. *Biomedical Ethics* (Opposing Viewpoints). San Diego, CA: Greenhaven Press, 1994.

Sherrow, Victoria. *Bioethics and High-Tech Medicine*. New York: Twenty-First Century Books, 1996.

Stwerka, Eve, and Albert Stwerka. *Genetic Engineering*. New York: Franklin Watts, 1982.

Vogel, Carole. *Will I Get Breast Cancer?* Parsipanny, NJ: Julian Messner, 1994.

Wilcox, Frank H. *DNA: The Thread of Life.* Minneapolis, MN: Lerner Publications Co., 1988.

Yont, Lisa. *Cancer.* San Diego, CA: Lucent Books, 1999.

St. Margaret Middle School Library
1716-A Churchville Road
Bel Air, Maryland 21015

Bibliography

Cook-Degan, Robert M. *The Gene Wars: Science, Politics, and the Human Genome.* New York: W. W. Norton & Co., 1994.

Cooper, Necia Grant, ed. *The Human Genome Project: Deciphering the Blueprint of Heredity.* Mill Valley, CA: University Science Books, 1994.

Dennis, Carina, and Richard Gallagher. *The Human Genome.* New York: Palgrave, 2001.

Jaroff, Leon. *The New Genetics.* Knoxville, TN: Whittle Direct Books, 1991.

Keveles, Daniel J., and Leroy Hood, eds. *The Code of Codes: Scientific and Social Issues in the Human Genome Project.* Cambridge, MA: Harvard University Press, 1992.

Lee, Thomas F. *The Human Genome Project: Cracking the Genetic Code of Life.* New York: Plenum Press, 1991.

Index

Credits

ABOUT THE AUTHOR

James Toriello has written several books for young readers, including three books in the Rosen Publishing Group's Holocaust Biographies series.

PHOTO CREDITS

Cover, p. 26 © Richard T. Nowitz/Corbis; cover inset (front and back), p. 1 © PhotoDisc, Getty Images; folio banners © EyeWire; pp. 4–5, 20–21 © Custom Medical Stock Photo, Inc.; p. 6 © O'Donnell/CMSP; pp. 8–9 © BSIP/Jacopin/Science Source.; p. 12 © Latin Stock Kairos/Photo Researchers, Inc.; p. 13 © Bettmann/Corbis; p. 16 © Roger Ressmeyer/Corbis; p. 18 © AFP/Corbis; pp. 30–31 © Jim Dowdalls/Photo Reseachers, Inc.; p. 34 © S. Miller/CMSP; p. 36 © Bob Child/AP Wide World Photos; p. 37 © M. Baret/Rapho/Photo Researchers, Inc.; pp. 40–41 © BSIP/CMSP; p. 44 © Breck Smither/AP Wide World Photos; pp. 48–49 © Imagineering/CMSP; p. 50 © Roger Ressmeyer/Corbis.

DESIGN AND LAYOUT

Evelyn Horovicz